OILS

by Tea Benduhn

Reading consultant: Susan Nations, M.Ed., author/literacy coach/
consultant in literacy development

WEEKLY READER®
PUBLISHING

Please visit our web site at: www.garethstevens.com
For a free color catalog describing our list of high-quality books,
call 1-800-542-2595 (USA) or 1-800-387-3178 (Canada).

Library of Congress Cataloging-in-Publication Data

Benduhn, Tea.
    Oils / by Tea Benduhn.
       p. cm. — (Find out about food)
    Includes bibliographical references and index.
    ISBN: 978-0-8368-8254-4 (lib. bdg.)
    ISBN: 978-0-8368-8261-2 (softcover)
    1. Oils and fats, Edible. I. Title.
  TX407.O34B46   2007
  664'.3—dc22   2007006048

This edition first published in 2008 by
Weekly Reader® Books
An imprint of Gareth Stevens Publishing
1 Reader's Digest Road
Pleasantville, NY 10570-7000 USA

Copyright © 2008 by Gareth Stevens, Inc.

Managing editor: Valerie J. Weber
Art direction: Tammy West
Graphic designer: Scott Krall
Picture research: Diane Laska-Swanke
Photographer: Gregg Andersen
Production: Jessica Yanke

Printed in the United States of America

1 2 3 4 5 6 7 8 9 11 10 09 08 07

Note to Educators and Parents

Reading is such an exciting adventure for young children! They are beginning to integrate their oral language skills with written language. To encourage children along the path to early literacy, books must be colorful, engaging, and interesting; they should invite the young reader to explore both the print and the pictures.

The *Find Out About Food* series is designed to help children understand the value of good nutrition and eating to stay healthy. In each book, young readers will learn how their favorite foods — and possibly some new ones — fit into a balanced diet.

Each book is specially designed to support the young reader in the reading process. The familiar topics are appealing to young children and invite them to read — and re-read — again and again. The full-color photographs and enhanced text further support the student during the reading process.

In addition to serving as wonderful picture books in schools, libraries, homes, and other places where children learn to love reading, these books are specifically intended to be read within an instructional guided reading group. This small group setting allows beginning readers to work with a fluent adult model as they make meaning from the text. After children develop fluency with the text and content, the book can be read independently. Children and adults alike will find these books supportive, engaging, and fun!

— Susan Nations, M.Ed., author, literacy coach,
and consultant in literacy development

My brother told me I should eat oils every day. I asked him why.

Oils are part of the **food pyramid**. The six colored bands on the food pyramid stand for types of foods. Make smart choices. Eat these foods and **exercise** every day.

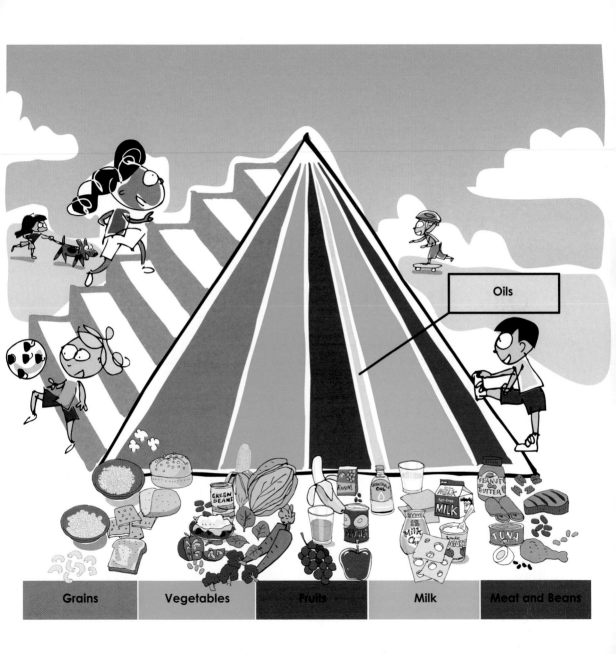

Oils

Grains   Vegetables   Fruits   Milk   Meat and Beans

The yellow band stands for oils. It is the thinnest band. The width means you should not eat a lot of oils.

Oils are part of many foods.
Some oils are good for you.
Nuts, olives, and fish have
good oils in them.

Some oils are bad for you. Butter has oil in it. Butter is not good for you. Many sweet treats are made with butter.

The good types of oils keep your skin **healthy**. They help your **muscles** stay strong, too. Healthy muscles help you stay **active**.

Some oils come from plants. We use **vegetable oil** at our house. My dad cooks with sunflower oil.

Oils are in other foods, too. Mom makes salad dressing with olive oil.

I already eat enough oils every day. I like to eat **almonds**. I eat fish, too. The same foods I eat every day will give me all the oils I need.